D0989584

A Child's First Book

about

PLAY THERAPY

Marc A. Nemiroff, PhD
and
Jane Annunziata, PsyD

Illustrated by Margaret Scott

AMERICAN PSYCHOLOGICAL ASSOCIATION

Washington, DC

The Library
Special Childrens Collection
Saint Francis College
Fort Wayne, Indiana

Copyright © 1990 by the American Psychological
Association. All rights reserved. Except as permitted
under the United States Copyright Act of 1976, no part of
this publication may be reproduced or distributed in
any form or by any means, or stored in a database or
retrieval system, without the prior written permission
of the publisher.

Fifth Printing July 1996

Published by
American Psychological Association
750 First Street, NE
Washington, DC 20002

Copies may be ordered from
APA Order Department
P.O. Box 2710
Hyattsville, MD 20784

In the United Kingdom and Europe, copies may be ordered from
American Psychological Association
3 Henrietta Street
Covent Garden
London WC2E 8LU
England

Illustrated by Margaret Scott
Typeset and printed by York Graphic Services, Inc.,
York, PA
Production coordinated by Valerie J. Montenegro

Library of Congress Cataloging-in-Publication Data

Nemiroff, Marc A.
    A child's first book about play therapy/Marc A.
    Nemiroff and Jane Annunziata.—1st ed.
        p.   cm.
    Summary: Readers learn about psychotherapy and
the value of play as treatment for behavior problems in
small children.
    ISBN 1-55798-112-4, casebound; 1-55798-089-6,
softcover
    1. Play therapy—Juvenile literature.   (1. Play
therapy.   2. Psychotherapy.)   I. Annunziata, Jane.
II. Title.
RJ505.P6N46   1990
618.92'891653—dc20   90-49954
                                            CIP
                                            AC

Printed in the United States of America

Note to Parents and Guardians

This book is intended for young children, ages 4 to 7 or so, for whom psychotherapy is being considered. You can read it to your child, or a child who reads can read it with your help.

There are often many questions about psychological treatment of a young child: What is play therapy? What happens in a session? How does it work? Why do children see a therapist? This book talks about the following issues that your child's therapist will have explained to you before treatment begins, or may explain to you as treatment progresses:

- things a child does that indicate a possible problem (what therapists call "presenting problems");
- how a child enters treatment (referral);
- confidentiality;
- the therapist's office and equipment;
- the activity of play therapy (what actually happens);
- how a child improves over time;
- how treatment will end (a particularly anxious period for children in treatment) and how a child's anxiety will sometimes cause him or her to temporarily return to problem behavior at that time (temporary regression).

We have tried to answer these questions from the viewpoint of the young patient. At the end of this book, you will find "Information for Parents and Guardians" that provides you with more detail about reasons for referral and where to go for help.

We hope that this book will address some of the worries your child (and you) may have at the beginning of treatment.

Marc A. Nemiroff
Jane Annunziata

Note to Mental Health Professionals

This book was written to facilitate entry into treatment of the young child (ages 4 to 7). Our intention was to create a tool that could be used to explain the process of play therapy to the young patient. We wrote the book because we believe there is a real value in speaking directly to the child in this way—and, because, after years of treating children in private and community mental health care settings, we could find no similar resource.

The book discusses many of the questions and concerns that children (and their parents or guardians) have about psychotherapy. The text reflects, in very simplified language, our psychodynamic approach to play therapy. We hope that it is written in a way that a child can understand, but says things that adults need to know, too.

You may wish to keep a copy of this brief book in your waiting room so that youngsters and adults can peruse it there. You may also wish to give it to parents and others after recommending psychotherapy for a child. Guidance counselors or special education teachers may find it particularly useful when referring a family to a child therapist. More fragile children may also be able to use it as a bridge between them and their therapists and find comfort in being able to read it between sessions.

For Gabriel and Bret
and
all the other children

Have you ever noticed how some kids have problems?

They might get into fights a lot.

They might have trouble sharing.

They might
feel very
shy and nervous
around
other kids.

Or maybe
they worry
a lot.

Doing one of these things
a lot means that kids have
problems.

A problem is a thing you
worry about or feel bad
about.

Sometimes a problem
makes you want to cry,

Or hit someone,

Or be all by

Yourself.

It's hard to keep having these problems. It bothers children. They don't know where the problems come from. So, they can't make them go away.

Then

They

Need

Help.

Sometimes a mom or dad can help.

But sometimes you need special help.

There are special kinds of
helpers for children
with these kinds of
problems.

Some people call them
"worry doctors," but
their real name is
child therapists.

(There's only one other big
word like "Therapist" in
this book.)

Child therapists help
children learn about the
worries and feelings
that make the problems
in the first place.

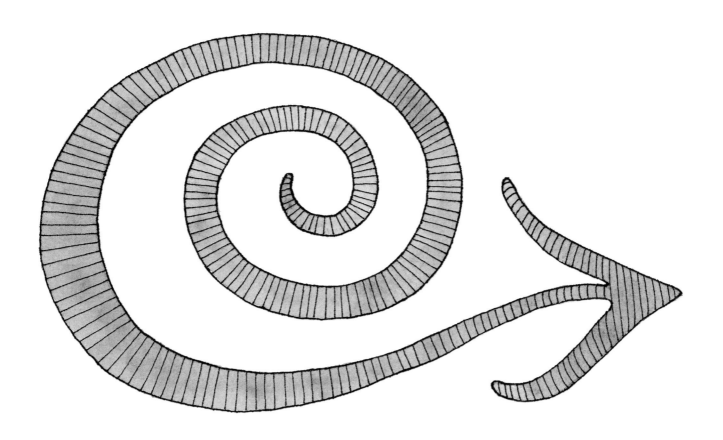

What happens when you visit a child therapist?

Will he talk like my teacher?

Will she give me shots like my regular doctor?

Will I
go all
by
myself?

First, the therapist will meet with your parents to find out about the problems.

Second, your parents
will bring you to see
the therapist.

Then your parents and the therapist will plan the best way to help you.

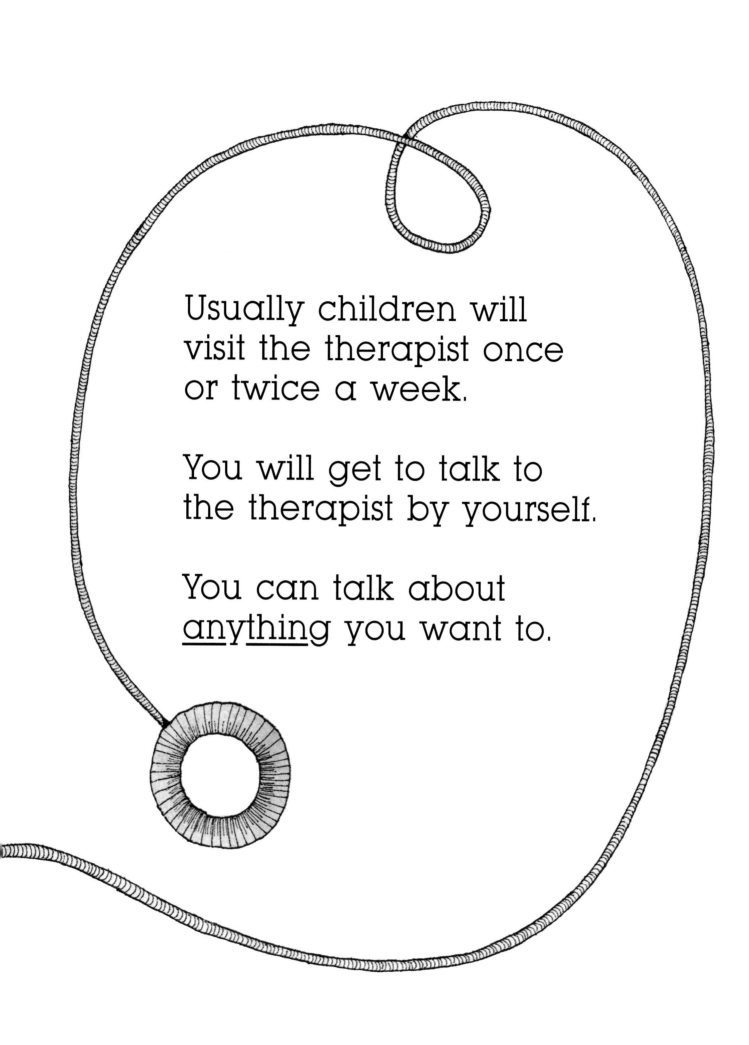

Usually children will
visit the therapist once
or twice a week.

You will get to talk to
the therapist by yourself.

You can talk about
<u>anything</u> you want to.

Every once in a while,
your mom and dad will
talk to the therapist.

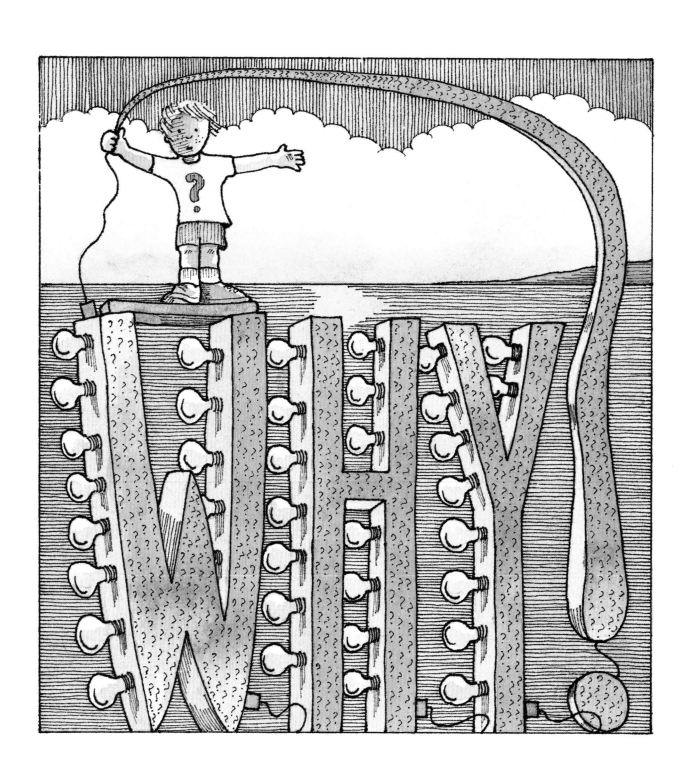

Children get better quicker when parents meet with the therapist, too.

They will help the therapist understand you. . . .

And the therapist will teach them new things to do when you have problems.

Do you remember
we said that you
can talk with
the therapist
about
ANYTHING
?

Well, there's something
important you need
to know about that. . . .

(Here comes the
other big word
we told you about.)

(Whew!)

Confidentiality is like a one-way secret.

Therapists don't tell anyone the ideas or feelings kids work on. They keep them private.

But

KIDS

can talk about
them if they
want to.

WHAT'S IN A THERAPIST'S OFFICE

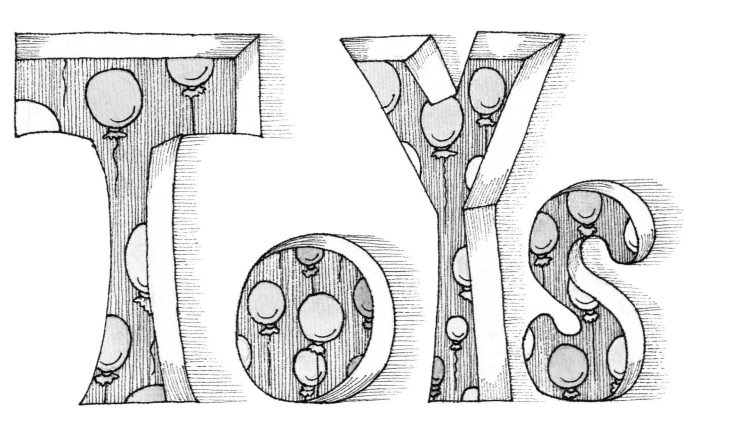

and art supplies
and some other
things, too.

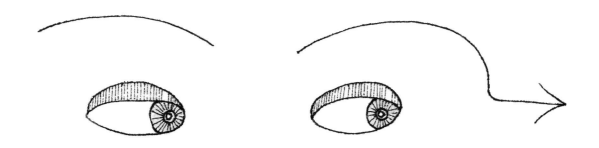

When kids play, the therapist can understand their feelings and their worries.

That's because children play their feelings better than they talk about them.

Child therapists help them understand their feelings while they play.

Children's problems seem to get better when they under-stand their feelings.

That's because kids sometimes have feelings they don't know they have.

So, how do they
find out about
these feelings?

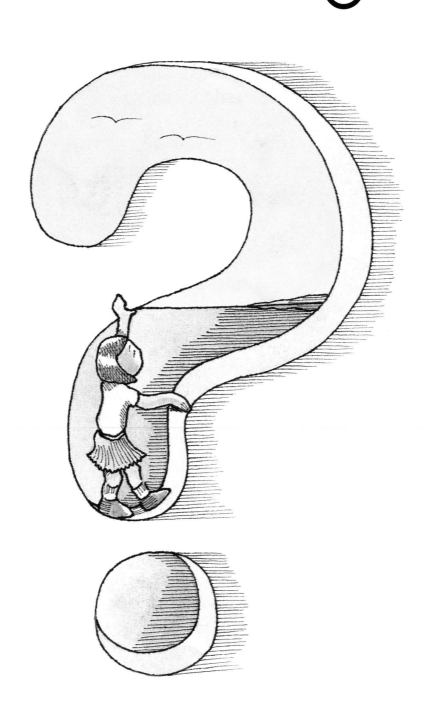

They
play

And
talk

And
draw...

And the therapist:

 Listens

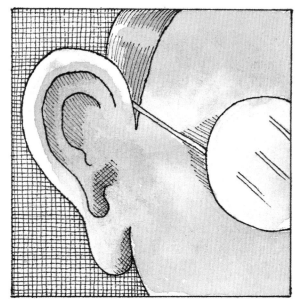

2. Watches

3. Under-
stands

 **4.** Sometimes plays, too

 **5.** Figures out the feelings and

 **6.** Talks with kids about them.

How do kids feel doing all this?

 Interested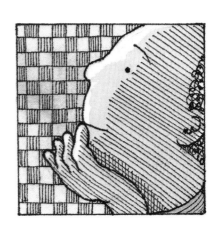

 Confused

 Sad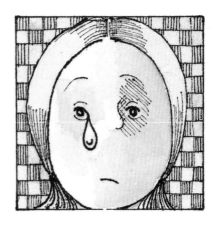

Mad

Glad

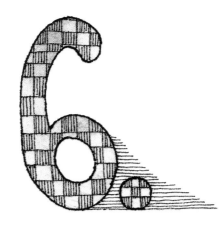

Lots of other feelings, too.

Therapists and kids talk and talk about these feelings. Sometimes it takes a long time.

And sometimes children
don't like to listen
to the therapist—

especially when
they are mad or
sad or confused.

Then, they don't like
what the therapist
has to say.

But that's okay . . .

Because the more kids talk about any of these feelings, their problems get smaller

and

smaller

and

smaller.

Getting better
is hard and it
takes a long
time.

But, finally,

kids

feel

nd then it's time to say, "goodbye." Saying goodbye to your therapist, who is your own special helper

G O O O O O O O O

and friend, can be hard, and scary, too.

This goodbye is different from other goodbyes because it's like saying a long goodbye.

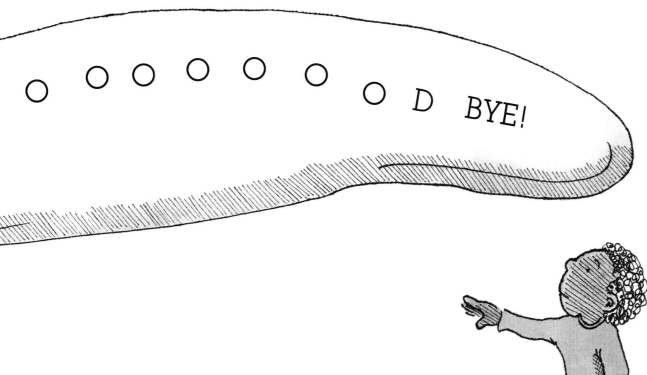

O O O O O O O D BYE!

Kids have some pretty important feelings to talk about at the end.

And, also, sometimes the problems come back a little.

But only for a short time.

This last part of therapy usually takes ———→

Here are some questions kids have at the end of therapy.

 Is my therapist going away?

No, your therapist will still be in the office. It's just that you won't be going anymore.

 Will I ever see my therapist again?

If you need to, your parents can call and arrange for you to visit.

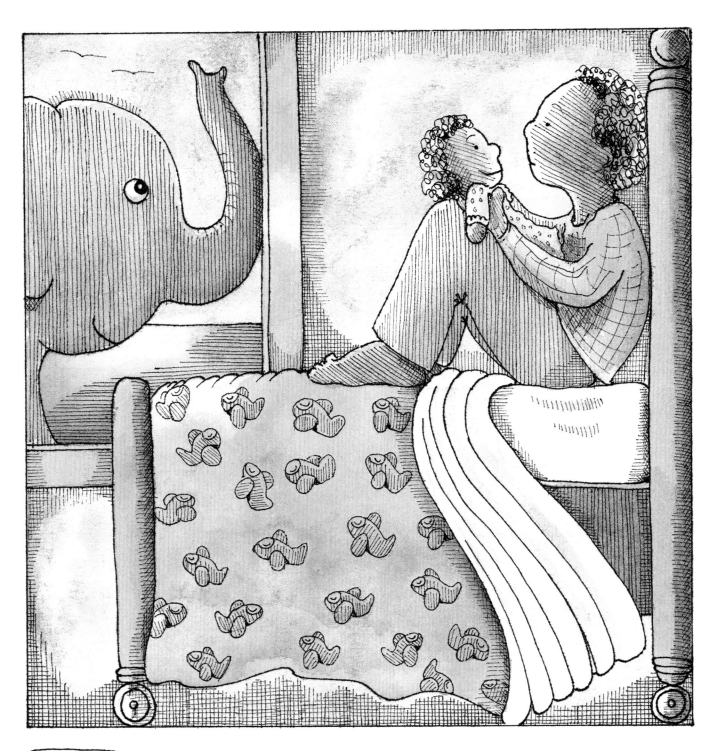

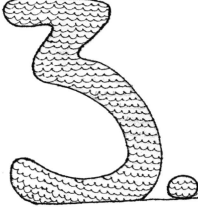

Will my
therapist
remember
me?

Information for Parents and Guardians

It is our experience that adults have questions about whether to seek psychotherapy for their children and where to go for help. We can offer the following general guidelines:

Does your child need therapy?

If your child appears to need help, the first step you should take is to consult with a mental health professional. The purpose of this initial consultation is to determine whether your child's individual difficulties do or do not require therapeutic intervention. Some of the factors that could be considered during the consultation are:

- How long has the problem persisted?
- Have attempts been made in the past to help the child overcome the problem? Did the child respond well but then return to the behavior or was the attempt unsuccessful?
- How disruptive is the problem to the child's daily functioning (that is, how serious is the problem)?
- Is the problem interfering with family life?
- Is the problem interfering with academic performance?
- Is the problem interfering with normal maturation?
- Is the problem unusual for the child's developmental stage?
- Is there only one problem, or is your child's visible (or presenting) problem one of a larger number of problems, some of which may not be immediately obvious?

Young children often show their distress directly and clearly through their behavior (such as becoming angry, hitting, crying, or displaying other kinds of pronounced behavior) or even by what they say. Sometimes, however, they communicate in more subtle ways. For example, children may become very quiet and withdrawn (a seemingly unproblematic behavior) or lethargic, may be reluctant to play with other children, or will show less imagination when they play.

If the therapist you consult with believes that there is a problem, he or she may recommend that your child enter treatment. The therapist may recommend a particular therapist by name or a particular kind of therapy.

You have a variety of choices regarding which type of professional your child sees. There are four major types of child therapists: psychiatrists, psychologists, social workers, and psychiatric nurses. These professionals have some of the same skills and training, but each type has unique areas of expertise. To find a therapist, ask advice from your child's pediatrician, guidance counselor, schoolteacher, the local mental health association, or a local community mental health center. One of these sources should be able to direct you to a professional with specialized training in work with children.

Don't be reluctant to "shop" for a child therapist. Asking questions and finding out whether you and your child will be comfortable with a therapist is the appropriate thing to do. Ask for several names when seeking a referral. Don't be afraid to ask about therapists' credentials and what to expect during treatment.

It's important for you to remember just how essential you are in helping the therapist help your child.

About the Authors

Marc A. Nemiroff has a PhD in clinical psychology from the Catholic University of America. Dr. Nemiroff has 16 years of experience in the treatment of children at the Woodburn Center for Community Mental Health in Annandale, Virginia, where he is the Coordinator of Youth and Family Programs. He is a member of the American Psychological Association, a fellow of the American Orthopsychiatric Association, and an affiliate member of the Baltimore-Washington Society for Psychoanalysis. Dr. Nemiroff maintains a private practice in Potomac, Maryland.

Jane Annunziata has a PsyD in clinical psychology from Rutgers University. She has taught at the University of Bergen (Norway), Mary Washington College, and George Mason University. For five years she was a member of the Children's Intensive Treatment Team at the Woodburn Center for Community Mental Health in Annandale, Virginia. Dr. Annunziata is in private practice in northern Virginia (McLean), where she specializes in work with children and their families as well as the individual treatment of adults.

The Library
Special Childrens Collection
Saint Francis College
Fort Wayne, Indiana